Rabindranath Tagore's The King Of The Dark Chamber

In this volume we venture to the East. To met a writer who speaks a common language of love and mysticism which continues to convey valuable insights into universal themes in contemporary society.

Rabindranath Tagore (1861-1941) who was a gifted Bengali Renaissance man, distinguishing himself as a philosopher, social and political reformer and a popular author in all literary genres. He was instrumental in an increased freedom for the press and influenced Gandhi and the founders of modern India.

He composed hundreds of songs which are still sung today as they include the Indian and Bangladeshi national anthems.

His prolific literary life has left a legacy of quality novels, essays, poems and in this volume one of his plays. He earned the distinction of being the first Asian writer to receive the Nobel Prize in Literature in 1913.

Many of his poems are also available as an audiobook from our sister company Portable Poetry as well as ebooks of stories and essays. Many samples are at our youtube channel
http://www.youtube.com/user/PortablePoetry?feature=mhee   The full volume of poems can be purchased from iTunes, Amazon and other digital stores. Among our readers are Shyama Perera and Ghizela Rowe

Index Of Contents
The King Of The Dark Chamber
Rabindranath Tagore – A Biography

The King Of The Dark Chamber

SCENE I

[A street. A few wayfarers, and a CITY GUARD]

FIRST MAN. Ho, Sir!

CITY GUARD. What do you want?

SECOND MAN. Which way should we go? We are strangers here. Please tell us which street we should take.

CITY GUARD. Where do you want to go?

THIRD MAN. To where those big festivities are going to be held, you know. Which way do we go?

CITY GUARD. One street is quite as good as another here. Any street will lead you there. Go straight ahead, and you cannot miss the place. [Exit.]

FIRST MAN. Just hear what the fool says: "Any street will lead you there!" Where, then, would be the sense of having so many streets?

SECOND MAN. You needn't be so awfully put out at that, my man. A country is free to arrange its affairs in its own way. As for roads in our country well, they are as good as non-existent; narrow and crooked lanes, a labyrinth of ruts and tracks. Our King does not believe in open thoroughfares; he thinks that streets are just so many openings for his subjects to fly away from his kingdom. It is quite the contrary here; nobody stands in your way, nobody objects to your going elsewhere if you like to; and yet the people are far from deserting this kingdom. With such streets our country would certainly have been depopulated in no time.

FIRST MAN. My dear Janardan, I have always noticed that this is a great fault in your character.

JANARDAN. What is?

FIRST MAN. That you are always having a fling at your country. How can you think that open highways may be good for a country? Look here, Kaundilya; here is a man who actually believes that open highways are the salvation of a country.

KAUNDILYA. There is no need, Bhavadatta, of my pointing out afresh that Janardan is blessed with an intelligence which is remarkably crooked, which is sure to land him in danger some day. If the King comes to hear of our worthy friend, he will make it a pretty hard job for him to find any one to do him his funeral rites when he is dead.

BHAVADATTA. One can't help feeling that life becomes a burden in this country; one misses the joys of privacy in these streets, this jostling and brushing shoulders with strange people day and night makes one long for a bath. And nobody can tell exactly what kind of people you are meeting with in these public roads, ugh!

KAUNDILYA. And it is Janardan who persuaded us to come to this precious country! We never had any second person like him in our family. You knew my father, of course; he was a great man, a pious man if ever there was one. He spent his whole life within a circle of a radius of 49 cubits drawn with a rigid adherence to the injunctions of the scriptures, and never for a single day did he cross this circle. After his death a serious difficulty arose, how cremate him within the limits of the 49 cubits and yet outside the house? At length the priests decided that though we could not go beyond the scriptural number, the only way out of the difficulty was to reverse the figure and make it 94 cubits; only thus could we cremate him outside the house without violating the sacred books. My word, that was strict observance! Ours is indeed no common country.

BHAVADATTA. And yet, though Janardan comes from the very same soil, he thinks it wise to declare that open highways are best for a country.

[Enter GRANDFATHER with a band of boys]

GRANDFATHER. Boys, we will have to vie with the wild breeze of the south to-day and we are not going to be beaten. We will sing till we have flooded all streets with our mirth and song.

SONG.

The southern gate is unbarred. Come, my spring, come!
Thou wilt swing at the swing of my heart, come, my spring, come!
Come in the lisping leaves, in the youthful surrender of flowers;
Come in the flute songs and the wistful sighs of the woodlands!
Let your unfastened robe wildly flap in the drunken wind!
Come, my spring, come!

[Exeunt.]

[Enter a band of CITIZENS]

FIRST CITIZEN. After all, one cannot help wishing that the King had allowed himself to be seen at least this one day. What a great pity, to live in his kingdom and yet not to have seen him for a single day!

SECOND CITIZEN. If you only knew the real meaning of all this mystery! I could tell you if you would keep a secret.

FIRST CITIZEN. My dear fellow, we both live in the same quarter of the town, but have you ever known me letting out any man s secret? Of course, that matter of your brother's finding a hidden fortune while digging for a well, well, you know well enough why I had to give it out. You know all the facts.

SECOND CITIZEN. Of course I know. And it is because I know that I ask, could you keep a secret if I tell you? It may mean ruination to us all, you know, if you once let it out.

THIRD CITIZEN. You are a nice man, after all, Virupaksha! Why are you so anxious to bring down a disaster which as yet only may happen? Who will be responsible for keeping your secret all his life?

VIRUPAKSHA. It is only because the topic came up, well, then, I shall not say anything. I am not the man to say things for nothing. You had yourself brought up the question that the King never showed himself; and I only remarked that it was not for nothing that the King shut himself up from the public gaze.

FIRST CITIZEN. Pray do tell us why, Virupaksha.

VIRUPAKSHA. Of course I don't mind telling you for we are all good friends, aren't we? There can be no harm. (With a low voice.) The King is hideous to look at, so he has made up his mind never to show himself to his subjects.

FIRST CITIZEN. Ha! that's it! It must be so. We have always wondered ... why, the mere sight of a King in all countries makes one's soul quake like an aspen leaf with fear; but why should our King never have been seen by any mortal soul? Even if he at least came out and consigned us all to the gibbet, we might be sure that our King was no hoax. After all, there is much in Virupaksha's explanation that sounds plausible enough.

THIRD CITIZEN. Not a bit, I don't believe in a syllable of it.

VIRUPAKSHA. What, Vishu, do you mean to say that I am a liar?

VISHU. I don't exactly mean that but I cannot accept your theory. Excuse me, I cannot help if I seem a bit rude or churlish.

VIRUPAKSHA. Small wonder that you can't believe my words, you who think yourself sage enough to reject the opinions of your parents and superiors. How long do you think you could have stayed in this country if the King did not remain in hiding? You are no better than a flagrant heretic.

VISHU. My dear pillar of orthodoxy! Do you think any other King would have hesitated to cut off your tongue and make it food for dogs? And you have the face to say that our King is horrid to look at!

VIRUPAKSHA. Look here, Vishu. will you curb your tongue?

VISHU. It would be superfluous to point out whose tongue needs the curbing.

FIRST CITIZEN. Hush, my dear friends, this looks rather bad.... It seems as if they are resolved to put me in danger as well. I am not going to be a party to all this.[Exit.]

[Enter a number of men, dragging in GRANDFATHER, in boisterous exuberance]

SECOND CITIZEN. Grandpa, something strikes me to-day ...

GRANDFATHER. What is it?

SECOND CITIZEN. This year every country has sent its people to our festival, but every one asks, "Everything is nice and beautiful but where is your King?" and we do not know what to answer. That is the one big gap which cannot but make itself felt to every one in our country.

GRANDFATHER. "Gap," do you say! Why, the whole country is all filled and crammed and packed with the King: and you call him a "gap"! Why, he has made every one of us a crowned King!

SINGS.

We are all Kings in the kingdom of our King.
Were it not so, how could we hope in our heart to meet him!
We do what we like, yet we do what he likes;
We are not bound with the chain of fear at the feet of a slave-owning King.
Were it not so, how could we hope in our heart to meet him!
Our King honours each one of us, thus honours his own very self.
No littleness can keep us shut up in its walls of untruth for aye.
Were it not so, how could we have hope in our heart to meet him!
We struggle and dig our own path, thus reach his path at the end.
We can never get lost in the abyss of dark night.
Were it not so, how could we hope in our heart to meet him!

THIRD CITIZEN. But, really, I cannot stand the absurd things people say about our King simply because he is not seen in public.

FIRST CITIZEN. Just fancy! Any one libelling me can be punished, while nobody can stop the mouth of any rascal who chooses to slander the King.

GRANDFATHER. The slander cannot touch the King. With a mere breath you can blow out the flame which a lamp inherits from the sun, but if all the world blow upon the sun itself its effulgence remains undimmed and unimpaired as before.

[Enter VISHVAVASU and VIRUPAKSHA]

VISHU. Here's Grandfather! Look here, this man is going about telling everybody that our King does not come out because he is ugly.

GRANDFATHER. But why does that make you angry, Vishu? His King must be ugly, because how else could Virupaksha possess such features in his kingdom? He fashions his King after the image of himself he sees in the mirror.

VIRUPAKSHA. Grandfather, I shall mention no names, but nobody would think of disbelieving the person who gave me the news.

GRANDFATHER. Who could be a higher authority than yourself!

VIRUPAKSHA. But I could give you proofs ...

FIRST CITIZEN. The impudence of this fellow knows no bounds! Not content with spreading a ghastly rumour with an unabashed face, he offers to measure his lies with insolence!

SECOND CITIZEN. Why not make him measure his length on the ground?

GRANDFATHER. Why so much heat, my friends? The poor fellow is going to have his own festive day by singing the ugliness of his King. Go along, Virupaksha, you will find plenty of people ready to believe you: may you be happy in their company.[Exeunt.]

[Re-enter the party of FOREIGNERS]

BHAVADATTA. It strikes me, Kaundilya, that these people haven't got a King at all. They have somehow managed to keep the rumour afloat.

KAUNDILYA. You are right, I think. We all know that the supreme thing that strikes one's eye in any country is the King, who of course loses no opportunity of exhibiting himself.

JANARDAN. But look at the nice order and regularity prevailing all over the place, how do you explain it without a King?

BHAVADATTA. So this is the wisdom you have arrived at by living so long under a ruler! Where would be the necessity of having a King if order and harmony existed already?

JANARDAN. All these people have assembled to rejoice at this festival. Do you think they could come together like this in a country of anarchy?

BHAVADATTA. My dear Janardan, you are evading the real issue, as usual. There can be no question about the order and regularity, and the festive rejoicing too is plain enough: there is no difficulty so far. But where is the King? Have you seen him? Just tell us that.

JANARDAN. What I want to say is this: you know from your experience that there can be chaos and anarchy even if a King be present: but what do we see here?

KAUNDILYA. You are always coming back to your quibbling. Why can you not give a straight answer to Bhavadatta's question. Have you, or have you not, seen the King? Yes or no? [Exeunt.]

[Enter a band of MEN, singing]

SONG.

My beloved is ever in my heart
That is why I see him everywhere,
He is in the pupils of my eyes
That is why I see him everywhere.
I went far away to hear his own words,
But, ah, it was vain!
When I came back I heard them
In my own songs.
Who are you who seek him like a beggar
from door to door!
Come to my heart and see his face in the
tears of my eyes!

[Enter HERALDS and ADVANCE GUARDS of the KING]

FIRST HERALD. Stand off! Get away from the street, all of you!

FIRST CITIZEN. Eh, man, who do you think you are? You weren't of course born with such lofty strides, my friend? Why should we stand off, my dear sir? Why should we budge? Are we street dogs, or what?

SECOND HERALD. Our King is coming this way.

SECOND CITIZEN. King? Which King?

FIRST HERALD. Our King, the King of this country.

FIRST CITIZEN. What, is the fellow mad? Whoever heard of our King coming out heralded by these vociferous gentry?

SECOND HERALD. The King will no longer deny himself to his subjects. He is coming to command the festivities himself.

SECOND CITIZEN. Brother, is that so?

SECOND HERALD. Look, his banner is flying over there.

SECOND CITIZEN. Ah, yes, that is a flag indeed.

SECOND HERALD. Do you see the red *Kimshuk* flower painted on it?

SECOND CITIZEN. Yes, yes, it is the *Kimshuk* indeed! what a bright scarlet flower!

FIRST HERALD. Well! do you believe us now?

SECOND CITIZEN. I never said I didn't. That fellow Kumbha started all this fuss. Did I say a word?

FIRST HERALD. Perhaps, though a pot-bellied man, he is quite empty inside; an empty vessel sounds most, you know.

SECOND HERALD. Who is he? Is he any kinsman of yours?

SECOND CITIZEN. Not at all. He is just a cousin of our village chief's father-in-law, and he does not even live in the same part of our village with us.

SECOND HERALD. Just so: he quite looks the seventh cousin of somebody's father-in-law, and his understanding appears also to bear the stamp of uncle-in-lawhood.

KUMBHA. Alas, my friends, many a bitter sorrow has given my poor mind a twist before it has become like this. It is only the other day that a King came and paraded the streets, with as many titles in front of him as the drums that made the town hideous by their din, ... What did I not do to serve and please him! I rained presents on him, I hung about him like a beggar and in the end I found the strain on my resources too hard to bear. But what was the end of all that pomp and majesty? When people sought grants and presents from him, he could not somehow discover an auspicious day in the Calendar: though all days were red-letter days when we had to pay our taxes!

SECOND HERALD. Do you mean to insinuate that our King is a bogus King like the one you have described?

FIRST HERALD. Mr. Uncle-in-law, I believe the time has come for you to say good-bye to Aunty-in-law.

KUMBHA. Please, sirs, do not take any offence. I am a poor creature, my sincerest apologies, sirs: I will do anything to be excused. I am quite willing to move away as far as you like.

SECOND HERALD. All right, come here and form a line. The King will come just now, we shall go and prepare the way for him. [They go out.]

SECOND CITIZEN. My dear Kumbha, your tongue will be your death one day.

KUMBHA. Friend Madhav, it isn't my tongue, it is fate. When the bogus King appeared I never said a word, though that did not prevent my striking at my own feet with all the self-confidence of innocence. And now, when perhaps the real King has come, I simply must blurt out treason. It is fate, my dear friend!

MADHAV. My faith is, to go on obeying the King, it does not matter whether he is a real one or a pretender. What do we know of Kings that we should judge them! It is like throwing stones in the dark, you are almost sure of hitting your mark. I go on obeying and acknowledging, if it is a real King, well and good: if not, what harm is there?

KUMBHA. I should not have minded if the stones were nothing better than stones. But they are often precious things: here, as elsewhere, extravagance lands us in poverty, my friend.

MADHAV. Look! There comes the King! Ah, a King indeed! What a figure, what a face! Whoever saw such beauty; lily-white, creamy-soft! What now, Kumbha? What do you think now?

KUMBHA. He looks all right, yes, he may be the real King for all I know.

MADHAV. He looks as if he were moulded and carved for kingship, a figure too exquisite and delicate for the common light of day.

[Enter the "KING"]

[Transcriber's note: The author indicates the trumped up King as "KING" in this play, enclosing the word King in double quotes to help us distinguish the imposter from the real one.]

MADHAV. Prosperity and victory attend thee, O King! We have been standing here to have a sight of thee since the early morning. Forget us not, your Majesty, in your favours.

KUMBHA. The mystery deepens. I will go and call Grandfather.[Goes out.]

[Enter another band of MEN]

FIRST MAN. The King, the King! Come along, quick, the King is passing this way.

SECOND MAN. Do not forget me, O King! I am Vivajadatta, the grandson of Udayadatta of Kushalivastu. I came here at the first report of thy coming, I did not stop to hear what people were saying: all the loyalty in me went out towards thee, O Monarch, and brought me here.

THIRD MAN. Rubbish! I came here earlier than you before the cockcrow. Where were you then? O King, I am Bhadrasena, of Vikramasthali. Deign to keep thy servant in thy memory!

"KING". I am much pleased with your loyalty and devotion.

VIVAJADATTA. Your Majesty, many are the grievances and complaints we have to make to thee: to whom could we turn our prayers so long, when we could not approach thy august presence?

"KING". Your grievances will all be redressed. [Exit.]

FIRST MAN. It won't do to lag behind, boys, the King will lose sight of us if we get mixed up with the mob.

SECOND MAN. See there-look what that fool Narottam is doing! He has elbowed his way through all of us and is now sedulously fanning the King with a palm leaf!

MADHAV. Indeed! Well, well, the sheer audacity of the man takes one's breath away.

SECOND MAN. We shall have to pitch the fellow out of that place, is he fit to stand beside the King?

MADHAV. Do you imagine the King will not see through him? His loyalty is obviously a little too showy and profuse.

FIRST MAN. Nonsense! Kings can't scent hypocrites as we do, I should not be surprised if the King be taken in by that fool's strenuous fanning.

[Enter KUMBHA with GRANDFATHER]

KUMBHA. I tell you he has just passed by this street.

GRANDFATHER. Is that a very infallible test of Kingship?

KUMBHA. Oh no, he did not pass unobserved: not one or two men but hundreds and thousands on both sides of the street have seen him with their own eyes.

GRANDFATHER. That is exactly what makes the whole affair suspicious. When ever has our King set out to dazzle the eyes of the people by pomp and pageantry? He is not the King to make such a thundering row over his progress through the country.

KUMBHA. But he may just have chosen to do so on this important occasion: you cannot really tell.

GRANDFATHER. Oh yes, you can! My King cherishes no weathercock fancy, no fantastic vein.

KUMBHA. But, Grandfather, I wish I could only describe him! So soft, so delicate and exquisite like a waxen doll! As I looked on him, I yearned to shelter him from the sun, to protect him with my whole body.

GRANDFATHER. Fool, O precious ass that you are! *My* King a waxen doll, and you to protect him!

KUMBHA. But seriously, Grandpa, he is a superb god, a miracle of beauty: I do not find a single other figure in this vast assembly that can stand beside his peerless loveliness.

GRANDFATHER. If my King chose to make himself shown, your eyes would not have noticed him. He would not stand out like that amongst others, he is one of the people, he mingles with the common populace.

KUMBHA. But did I not tell you I saw his banner?

GRANDFATHER. What did you see displayed on his banner?

KUMBHA. It had a red *Kimshuk* flower painted on it, the bright and glittering scarlet dazzled my eyes.

GRANDFATHER. *My* King has a thunderbolt within a lotus painted on his flag.

KUMBHA. But every one is saying, the King is out in this festival: *every one*.

GRANDFATHER. Why, so he is, of course: but he has no heralds, no army, no retinue, no music bands or lights to accompany him.

KUMBHA. So none could recognise him in his incognito, it seems.

GRANDFATHER. Perhaps there are a few that can.

KUMBHA. And those that can recognise him, does the King grant them whatever they ask for?

GRANDFATHER. But they never ask for anything. No beggar will ever know the King. The greater beggar appears like the King to the eyes of the lesser beggar. O fool, the man that has come out to-day attired in crimson and gold to beg from you, it is him whom you are trumpeting as your King! ... Ah, there comes my mad friend! Oh come, my brothers! we cannot spend the day in idle wrangling and prating, let us now have some mad frolic, some wild enjoyment!

[Enter the MAD FRIEND, who sings]

Do you smile, my friends? Do you laugh, my brothers? I roam in search of the golden stag! Ah yes, the fleet-foot vision that ever eludes me!

Oh, he flits and glimpses like a flash and then is gone, the untamed rover of the wilds! Approach him and he is afar in a trice, leaving a cloud of haze and dust before thy eyes!

Yet I roam in search of the golden stag, though I may never catch him in these wilds! Oh, I roam and wander through woods and fields and nameless lands like a restless vagabond, never caring to turn my back.

You all come and buy in the marketplace and go back to your homes laden with goods and provisions: but me the wild winds of unscalable heights have touched and kissed, Oh, I know not when or where!

I have parted with my all to get what never has become mine! And yet think my moanings and my tears are for the things I thus have lost!

With a laugh and a song in my heart I have left all sorrow and grief far behind me: Oh, I roam and wander through woods and fields and nameless lands, never caring to turn my vagabond's back!

SCENE II

[A DarkChamber. QUEEN SUDARSHANA. Her Maid of Honour, SURANGAMA]

SUDARSHANA. Light, light! Where is light? Will the lamp never be lighted in this chamber?

SURANGAMA. My Queen, all your other rooms are lighted, will you never long to escape from the light into a dark room like this?

SUDARSHANA. But why should this room be kept dark?

SURANGAMA. Because otherwise you would know neither light nor darkness.

SUDARSHANA. Living in this dark room you have grown to speak darkly and strangely, I cannot understand you, Surangama. But tell me, in what part of the palace is this chamber situated? I cannot make out either the entrance or the way out of this room.

SURANGAMA. This room is placed deep down, in the very heart of the earth. The King has built this room specially for your sake.

SUDARSHANA. Why, he has no dearth of rooms, why need he have made this chamber of darkness specially for me?

SURANGAMA. You can meet others in the lighted rooms: but only in this dark room can you meet your lord.

SUDARSHANA. No, no, I cannot live without light, I am restless in this stifling dark. Surangama, if you can bring a light into this room, I shall give you this necklace of mine.

SURANGAMA. It is not in my power, O Queen. How can I bring light to a place which he would have kept always dark!

SUDARSHANA. Strange devotion! And yet, is it not true that the King punished your father?

SURANGAMA. Yes, that is true. My father used to gamble. All the young men of the country used to gather at my father's house-and they used to drink and gamble.

SUDARSHANA. And when the King sent away your father in exile, did it not make you feel bitterly oppressed?

SURANGAMA. Oh, it made me quite furious. I was on the road to ruin and destruction: when that path was closed for me, I seemed left without any support, without any succour or shelter. I raged and raved like a wild beast in a cage, how I wanted to tear every one to pieces in my powerless anger!

SUDARSHANA. But how did you get this devotion towards that same King?

SURANGAMA . How can I tell? Perhaps I could rely and depend on him because he was so hard, so pitiless!

SUDARSHANA. When did this change of feeling take place?

SURANGAMA. I could not tell you, I do not know that myself. A day came when all the rebel in me knew itself beaten, and then my whole nature bowed down in humble resignation on the dust of the earth. And then I saw ... I saw that he was as matchless in beauty as in terror. Oh. I was saved, I was rescued.

SUDARSHANA. Tell me, Surangama, I implore you, won't you tell me what is the King like to look at? I have not seen him yet for a single day. He comes to me in darkness, and leaves me in this dark room again. How many people have I not asked but they all return vague and dark answers, it seems to me that they all keep back something.

SURANGAMA. To tell you the truth, Queen, I could not say well what he is like. No, he is not what men call handsome.

SUDARSHANA. You don't say so? Not handsome!

SURANGAMA. No, my Queen, he is not handsome. To call him beautiful would be to say far too little about him.

SUDARSHANA. All your words are like that, dark, strange, and vague. I cannot understand what you mean.

SURANGAMA. No, I will not call him handsome. And it is because he is not beautiful that he is so wonderful, so superb, so miraculous!

SUDARSHANA. I do not quite understand you though I like to hear you talk about him. But I must see him at any cost. I do not even remember the day when I was married to him. I have heard mother say that a wise man came before my marriage and said, "He who will wed your daughter is without a second on this earth." How often have I asked her to describe his appearance to me, but she only answers vaguely, and says she cannot say she saw him through a veil, faintly and obscurely. But if he is the best among men, how can I sit still without seeing him?

SURANGAMA. Do you not feel a faint breeze blowing?

SUDARSHANA. A breeze? Where?

SURANGAMA. Do you not smell a soft perfume?

SUDARSHANA. No, I don't.

SURANGAMA. The large door has opened ... he is coming; my King is coming in.

SUDARSHANA. How can you perceive when he comes?

SURANGAMA. I cannot say: I seem to hear his footsteps in my own heart. Being his servant of this dark chamber, I have developed a sense, I can know and feel without seeing.

SUDARSHANA. Would that I had this sense too, Surangama!

SURANGAMA. You will have it, O Queen ... this sense will awaken in you one day. Your longing to have a sight of him makes you restless, and therefore all your mind is strained and warped in that direction. When you are past this state of feverish restlessness, everything will become quite easy.

SUDARSHANA. How is it that it is easy to you, who are a servant, and so difficult to me, the Queen?

SURANGAMA. It is because I am a mere servant that no difficulty baulks me. On the first day, when he left this room to my care, saying, "Surangama, you will always keep this chamber ready for me: this is all your task," then I did not say, even in thought, "Oh, give me the work of those who keep the other rooms lighted." No, but as soon as I bent all my mind to my task, a power woke and grew within me, and mastered every part of me unopposed.... Oh, there he comes! ... he is standing outside, before the door. Lord! O King!

SONG outside.

Open your door. I am waiting.
The ferry of the light from the dawn to the dark is done for
the day,
The evening star is up.
Have you gathered your flowers, braided your hair,
And donned your white robe for the night?
The cattle have come to their folds and birds to their nests.
The cross paths that run to all quarters have merged into one
in the dark.
Open your door. I am waiting.

SURANGAMA. O King, who can keep thy own doors shut against thee? They are not locked or bolted they will swing wide open if you only touch them with thy fingers. Wilt thou not even touch them? Wilt thou not enter unless I go and open the doors?

SONG.

At a breath you can remove my veils, my lord!
If I fall asleep on the dust and hear not your call, would you wait till I

wake?
Would not the thunder of your chariot wheel make the earth tremble? Would you not burst open the door and enter your own house unbidden?

Then do you go, O Queen, and open the door for him: he will not enter otherwise.

SUDARSHANA. I do not see anything distinctly in the dark, I do not know where the doors are. You know everything here, go and open the doors for me.

[SURANGAMA opens the door, bows to the KING, and goes out. The KING will remain invisible throughout this play.]

SUDARSHANA. Why do you not allow me to see you in the light?

KING. So you want to see me in the midst of a thousand things in broad daylight! Why should I not be the only thing you can feel in this darkness?

SUDARSHANA. But I must see you, I am longing to have a sight of you.

KING. You will not be able to bear the sight of me, it will only give you pain, poignant and overpowering.

SUDARSHANA. How can you say that I shall be unable to bear your sight? Oh, I can feel even in this dark how lovely and wonderful you are: why should I be afraid of you in the light? But tell me, can you see me in the dark?

KING. Yes, I can.

SUDARSHANA. What do you see?

KING. I see that the darkness of the infinite heavens, whirled into life and being by the power of my love, has drawn the light of a myriad stars into itself, and incarnated itself in a form of flesh and blood. And in that form, what aeons of thought and striving, untold yearnings of limitless skies, the countless gifts of unnumbered seasons!

SUDARSHANA. Am I so wonderful, so beautiful? When I hear you speak so, my heart swells with gladness and pride. But how can I believe the wonderful things you tell me? I cannot find them in myself!

KING. Your own mirror will not reflect them, it lessens you, limits you, makes you look small and insignificant. But could you see yourself mirrored in my own mind, how grand would you appear! In my own heart you are no longer the daily individual which you think you are, you are verily my second self.

SUDARSHANA. Oh, do show me for an instant how to see with your eyes! Is there nothing at all like darkness to you? I am afraid when I think of this. This darkness which is to me real and strong as death is this simply nothing to you? Then how can there be any union at all between us, in a place like this? No, no, it is impossible: there is a barrier betwixt us two: not here, no, not in this place. I want to find you and see you where I see trees and animals, birds and stones and the earth

KING. Very well, you can try to find me but none will point me out to you. You will have to recognise me, if you can, yourself. And even if anybody professes to show me to you, how can you be sure he is speaking the truth?

SUDARSHANA. I shall know you; I shall recognise you. I shall find you out among a million men. I cannot be mistaken.

KING. Very well, then, to-night, during the festival of the full moon of the spring, you will try to find me out from the high turret of my palace, search for me with your own eyes amongst the crowd of people.

SUDARSHANA. Wilt thou be there among them?

KING. I shall show myself again and again, from every side of the crowd. Surangama!

[Enter SURANGAMA]

SURANGAMA. What is thy pleasure, lord?

KING. To-night is the full moon festival of the spring.

SURANGAMA. What have I to do to-night?

KING. To-day is a festive day, not a day of work. The pleasure gardens are in their full bloom, you will join in my festivities there.

SURANGAMA. I shall do as thou desirest, lord.

KING. The Queen wants to see me to-night with her own eyes.

SURANGAMA. Where will the Queen see you?

KING. Where the music will play at its sweetest, where the air will be heavy with the dust of flowers, there in the pleasure grove of silver light and mellow gloom.

SURANGAMA. What can be seen in the hide-and-seek of darkness and light? There the wind is wild and restless, everything is dance and swift movement, will it not puzzle the eyes?

KING. The Queen is curious to search me out.

SURANGAMA. Curiosity will have to come back baffled and in tears!

SONG.

Ah, they would fly away, the restless vagrant eyes, the wild birds of the forest!
But the time of their surrender will come, their flights hither and thither will be ended when
The music of enchantment will pursue them and pierce their hearts.
Alas, the wild birds would fly to the wilderness!

SCENE III

[Before the Pleasure Gardens. Enter AVANTI, KOSHALA, KANCHI, and other KINGS]

AVANTI. Will the King of this place not receive us?

KANCHI. What manner of governing a country is this? The King is having a festival in a forest, where even the meanest and commonest people can have easy access!

KOSHALA. We ought to have had a separate place set apart and ready for our reception.

KANCHI. If he has not prepared such a place yet, we shall compel him to have one erected for us.

KOSHALA. All this makes one naturally suspect if these people have really got any King at all, it looks as if an unfounded rumour has led us astray.

AVANTI. It may be so with regard to the King, but the Queen Sudarshana of this place isn't at all an unfounded rumour.

KOSHALA. It is only for her sake that I have cared to come at all. I don't mind omitting to see one who never makes himself visible, but it would be a stupid mistake if we were to go away without a sight of one who is eminently worth a visit.

KANCHI. Let us make some definite plan, then.

AVANTI. A plan is an excellent thing, so long as you are not yourself entangled in it.

KANCHI. Hang it, who are these vermin swarming this way? Here! who are you?

[Enter GRANDFATHER and the boys]

GRANDFATHER. We are the Jolly Band of Have-Nothings.

AVANTI. The introduction was superfluous. But you will take yourselves away a little further and leave us in peace.

GRANDFATHER. We never suffer from a want of space: we can afford to give you as wide a berth as you like. What little suffices for us is never the bone of contention between any rival claimants. Is not that so, my little friends? [They sing.]

SONG.

We have nothing, indeed we have nothing at all!
We sing merrily fol de rol de rol!
Some build high walls of their houses
On the bog of the sands of gold.
We stand before them and sing
Fol de rol de rol.
Pickpockets hover about us
And honour us with covetous glances.
We shake our empty pockets and sing
Fol de rol de rol.
When death, the old hag, steals to our doors
We snap our fingers at her face,
And we sing in a chorus with gay flourishes
Fol de rol de rol.

KANCHI. Look over there, Koshala, who are those coming this way? A pantomime? Somebody is out masquerading as a King.

KOSHALA. The King of this place may tolerate all this tomfoolery, but we won't.

AVANTI. He is perhaps some rural chief.

[Enter GUARDS on foot]

KANCHI. What country does your King come from?

FIRST SOLDIER. He is the King of this country. He is going to command the festivities. [They go out.]

KOSHALA. What! The King of this country come out for the festivities!

AVANTI. Indeed! We shall then have to return with a sight of him only, leaving the delectable Queen unseen.

KANCHI. Do you really think that fellow spoke the truth? Anybody can pass himself off as the King of this kingless country. Can you not see that the man looks like a dressed-up King, much too over-dressed?

AVANTI. But he looks handsome, his appearance is not without a certain pleasing attractiveness.

KANCHI. He may be pleasing to your eye, but if you look at him closely enough there can be no mistaking him . You will see how I expose him before you all.

[Enter the trumped-up "KING".]

"KING". Welcome, princes, to our kingdom! I trust your reception has been properly looked after by my officials?

KINGS. [with feigned courtesy] Oh yes, nothing was lacking in the reception.

KANCHI. If there was any shortcoming at all, it has been made up by the honour of our sight of your Majesty.

"KING". We do not show ourselves to the general public, but your great devotion and loyalty to us has made it a pleasure for us not to deny ourselves to you.

KANCHI. It is truly hard for us, your Majesty, to bear the weight of your gracious favours.

"KING". We are afraid we shall not be able to stop here long.

KANCHI. I have thought so, already: you do not quite look up to it.

"KING". In the meantime if you have any favours to ask of us

KANCHI. We have: but we would like to speak a little more in private.

"KING". [to his attendants] Retire a little from our presence. [They retire.] Now you can express your desires without any reserve.

KANCHI. There will be no reserve on our part, our only fear is that you might think restraint necessary for yourself.

"KING". Oh no, you need have no scruples on that score.

KANCHI. Come, then, do us homage by placing your head on the ground before us.

"KING". It seems my servants have distributed the Varuni spirits too liberally in the reception camps.

KANCHI. False pretender, it is you who are suffering from an overdose of arrogant spirits. Your head will soon kiss the dust.

"KING". Princes, these heavy jokes are not worthy of a king.

KANCHI. Those who will jest properly with you are near at hand. General!

"KING". No more, I entreat you. I can see plainly I owe homage to you all. The head is bowing down of itself, there is no need for the application of any sharp methods to lay it low. So here I do my obeisance to you all. If you kindly allow me to escape I shall not inflict my presence long on you.

KANCHI. Why should you escape? We will make you king of this place, let us carry our joke to its legitimate finish. Have you got any following?

"KING". I have. Every one who sees me in the streets flocks after me. When I had a meagre retinue at first every one regarded me with suspicion, but now with the increasing crowd their doubts are waning and dissolving. The crowd is being hypnotised by its own magnitude. I have not got to do anything now.

KANCHI. That's excellent! From this moment we all promise to help and stand by you. But you will have to do us one service in return.

"KING". Your commands and the crown you are putting on my head will be equally binding and sacred to me.

KANCHI. At present we want nothing more than a sight of the Queen Sudarshana. You will have to see to this.

"KING". I shall spare no pains for that.

KANCHI. We cannot put much faith on your pains, you will be solely directed by our instructions. But now you can go and join the festivities in the royal arbour with all possible splendour and magnificence.[They go out.]

[Enter GRANDFATHER and a band of people]

FIRST CITIZEN. Grandfather, I cannot help saying yes, and repeating it five hundred times that our King is a perfect fraud.

GRANDFATHER. Why only five hundred times? There is no need to practise such heroic self-control, you can say it five thousand times if that adds to your pleasure.

SECOND CITIZEN. But you cannot keep up a dead lie forever.

GRANDFATHER. It has made me alive, my friend.

THIRD CITIZEN. We shall proclaim to the whole world that our King is a lie, the merest and emptiest shadow!

FIRST CITIZEN. We shall all shout from our housetops that we have no King, let him do whatever he likes if he exists.

GRANDFATHER. He will do nothing at all.

SECOND CITIZEN. My son died untimely at twenty-five of raging fever in seven days. Could such a calamity befall me under the rule of a virtuous King?

GRANDFATHER. But you still have got two sons left: while I have lost all my five children one after another.

THIRD CITIZEN. What do you say now?

GRANDFATHER. What then? Shall I lose my King too because I have lost my children? Don't take me for such a big fool as that.

FIRST CITIZEN. It is a fine thing to argue whether there is a King or not when one is simply starving for want of food! Will the King save us?

GRANDFATHER. Brother, you are right. But why not *find* the King who owns all the food? You certainly will not find by your wailings at home.

SECOND CITIZEN. Look at the justice of our King! That Bhadrasen, you know what a touching sight he is when he is speaking of his King, the sentimental idiot! He is reduced to such a state of penury that even the bats that infest his house find it a too uncomfortable place.

GRANDFATHER. Why, look at me! I am toiling and slaving night and day for my King, but I have not yet received so much as a brass farthing for my pains.

THIRD CITIZEN. Now, what do you think of that?

GRANDFATHER. What should I think? Does any one reward his friends? Go, my friends, and say if you like that our King exists nowhere. That is also a part of our ceremony in celebrating this festival.

SCENE IV

[Turret of the Royal Palace. SUDARSHANA and her friend ROHINI]

SUDARSHANA. You may make mistakes, Rohini, but I cannot be mistaken: am I not the Queen? That, of course, must be my King.

ROHINI. He who has conferred such high honour upon you cannot be long in showing himself to you.

SUDARSHANA. His very form makes me restless like a caged bird. Did you try well to ascertain who he is?

ROHINI. Yes, I did. Every one I asked said that he was the King.

SUDARSHANA. What country is he the King of?

ROHINI. Our country, King of this land.

SUDARSHANA. Are you sure that you are speaking of him who has a sunshade made of flowers held over his head?

ROHINI. The same: he whose flag has the *Kimshuk* flower painted on it.

SUDARSHANA. I recognised him at once, of course, but it is you who had your doubts.

ROHINI. We are apt to make mistakes, my Queen, and we are afraid to offend you in case we are wrong.

SUDARSHANA. Would that Surangama were here! There would remain no room for doubt then.

ROHINI. Do you think her cleverer than any of us?

SUDARSHANA. Oh no, but she would recognise him instantly.

ROHINI. I cannot believe that she would. She merely pretends to know him. There is none to test her knowledge if she professes to know the

King. If we were as shameless as she is, it would not have been difficult for us to boast about our acquaintance with the King.

SUDARSHANA. But no, she never boasts.

ROHINI. It is pure affectation, the whole of it: which often goes a longer way than open boasting. She is up to all manner of tricks: that is why we could never like her.

SUDARSHANA. But whatever you may say, I should have liked to ask her if she were here.

ROHINI. Very well, Queen. I shall bring her here. She must be lucky if she is indispensable for the Queen to know the King.

SUDARSHANA. Oh no, it isn't for that but I would like to hear it said by every one.

ROHINI. Is not every one saying it? Why, just listen, the acclamations of the people mount up even to this height!

SUDARSHANA. Then do one thing: put these flowers on a lotus leaf, and take them to him.

ROHINI. And what am I to say if he asks who sends them?

SUDARSHANA. You will not have to say anything, he will know. He thought that I would not be able to recognise him: I cannot let him off without showing that I have found him out. [ROHINI goes out with the flowers.]

SUDARSHANA. My heart is all a-quiver and restless to-night: I have never felt like this before. The white, silver light of the full moon is flooding the heavens and brimming over on every side like the bubbling foam of wine, ... It seizes on me like a yearning, like a mantling intoxication. Here, who is here?

[Enter a SERVANT]

SERVANT. What is your pleasure, your Majesty?

SUDARSHANA. Do you see those festive boys singing and moving through the alleys and avenues of the mango trees? Call them hither, bring them to me: I want to hear them sing. [SERVANT goes out and enters with the boys.] Come, living emblems of youthful spring, begin your festive song! All my mind and body is song and music to-night but the ineffable melody escapes my tongue: do you then sing for my sake!

SONG.

My sorrow is sweet to me in this spring night.
My pain smites at the chords of my love and softly sings.
Visions take birth from my yearning eyes and flit in the moonlit sky.
The smells from the depths of the woodlands have lost their way in my dreams.
Words come in whispers to my ears, I know not from where,
And bells in my anklets tremble and jingle in time with my heart thrills.

SUDARSHANA. Enough, enough, I cannot bear it any more! Your song has filled my eyes with tears.... A fancy comes to me that desire can never attain its object, it need never attain it. What sweet hermit of the woods has taught you this song? Oh that my eyes could see him whose song my ears have heard! Oh, how I wish, I wish I could wander rapt and lovely in the thick woodland arbours of the heart! Dear boys of the hermitage! how shall I reward you? This necklace is but made of jewels, hard stones, its hardness will give you pain, I have got nothing like the garlands of flowers you have on. [The boys bow and go out.]

[Enter ROHINI]

SUDARSHANA. I have not done well, I have not done well, Rohini. I feel ashamed to ask you what happened. I have just realised that no hand can really give the greatest of gifts. Still, let me hear all.

ROHINI. When I gave the King those flowers, he did not appear to understand anything.

SUDARSHANA. You don't say so? He did not understand

ROHINI. No; he sat there like a doll, without uttering a single word. I think he did not want to show that he understood nothing, so he just held his tongue.

SUDARSHANA. Fie on me! My shamelessness has been justly punished. Why did you not bring back my flowers?

ROHINI. How could I? The King of Kanchi, a very clever man, who was sitting by him, took in everything at a glance, and he just smiled a bit and said, "Emperor, the Queen Sudarshana sends your Majesty her greetings with these blossoms, the blossoms that belong to the God of Love, the friend of Spring." The King seemed to awake with a start, and said, "This is the crown of all my regal glory to-night." I was coming back, all out of countenance, when the King of Kanchi took off this necklace of jewels from the King's person, and said to me, "Friend, the King's garland gives itself up to you, in return for the happy fortune you have brought."

SUDARSHANA. What, Kanchi had to make the King understand all this! Woe is me, to-night's festival has opened wide for me the doors of ignominy and shame! What else could I expect? Leave me alone, Rohini; I want solitude for a time. [ROHINI goes out.] A great blow has shattered my pride to atoms to-day, and yet ... I cannot efface from my mind that beautiful, fascinating figure! No pride is left me, I am beaten, vanquished, utterly helpless.... I cannot even turn away from him. Oh, how the wish comes back to me again and again, to ask that garland of Rohini! But what would she think! Rohini!

[Enter ROHINI]

ROHINI. What is your wish?

SUDARSHANA. What reward do you deserve for your services to-day?

ROHINI. Nothing from you but I had my reward from the King as it should be.

SUDARSHANA. That is no free gift, but an extortion, of reward. I do not like to see you put on what was given in so indifferent a manner. Take it off, I give you my bracelets if you leave it here. Take these bracelets, and go now. [ROHINI goes out.] Another defeat! I should have thrown this necklace away, but I could not! It is pricking me as if it were a garland of thorns but I cannot throw it away. This is what the god of the festival has brought me to-night, this necklace of ignominy and shame!

SCENE V

[GRANDFATHER near the door of the Pleasure House. A Company of MEN]

GRANDFATHER. Have you had enough of it, friends?

FIRST MAN. Oh, more than that, Grandpa. Just see, they have made me red all over. None has escaped.

[Author's note: During the spring festival in India people throw red powder on each other. In this play this red powder has been taken to be the symbol of the passion of love.]

GRANDFATHER. No? Did they throw the red dust on the Kings too?

SECOND MAN. But who could approach them? They were all secure inside the enclosures.

GRANDFATHER. So they have escaped you! Could you not throw the least bit of colour on them? You should have forced your way there.

THIRD MAN. My dear old man, they have a different sort of red specially to themselves. Their eyes are red: the turbans of their guards and retinue are red too. And the latter flourished their swords about so much that a little more nearness on our part would have meant a lavish display of the fundamental red colour.

GRANDFATHER. Well done, friends, always keep them at a distance. They are the exiles of the Earth, and we have got to keep them so.

THIRD MAN. I am going home, Grandpa; it is past midnight.[Goes out.]

[Enter a BAND of SINGERS, singing.]

All blacks and whites have lost their distinction
And have become red, red as the tinge of your feet.
Red is my bodice and red are my dreams,
My heart sways and trembles like a red lotus.

GRANDFATHER. Excellent, my friends, splendid! So you had a really enjoyable time!

SINGERS. Oh, grand! Everything was red, red! Only the moon in the sky gave us the slip, it remained white.

GRANDFATHER. He only looks so innocent from the outside. If you had only taken off his white disguise, you would have seen his trickery. I have been watching what red colours he is throwing on the Earth to-night. And yet, fancy his remaining white and colourless all the while!

SONG.

With you is my game, love, my love!
My heart is mad, it will never own defeat,
Do you think you will escape stainless yourself reddening me with red powder?
Could I not colour your robe with the red pollens of the blossom of my heart?

[They go out.]

[Enter the "KING" and KANCHI.]

KANCHI. You must do exactly as I have told you. Let there be no mistake of any kind.

"KING". There shall be no mistake.

KANCHI. The Queen Sudarshana's mansions are in the ...

"KING". Yes, sire, I have seen the place well.

KANCHI. What you have got to do is to set fire to the garden, and then you will take advantage of the bustle and confusion to accomplish your object straightway.

"KING". I shall remember.

KANCHI. Look here, Sir Pretender, I cannot help thinking that a needless fear is troubling us, there is really no King in this country.

"KING". My sole aim is to rid this country of this anarchy. Your common man cannot live without a King, whether a real one or a fraud! Anarchy is always a source of danger.

KANCHI. Pious benefactor of the people, your wonderful self-sacrifice should really be an example to all of us. I am thinking of doing this extraordinary service to the people myself. [They go out.]

SCENE VI

ROHINI. What is the matter? I cannot make out what is all this! [To the GARDENERS.] Where are you all going away in such a hurry?

FIRST GARDENER. We are going out of the garden.

ROHINI. Where?

SECOND GARDENER. We do not know where the King has called us.

ROHINI. Why, the King is in the garden. Which King has called you?

FIRST GARDENER. We cannot say.

SECOND GARDENER. The King we have been serving all our life, of course.

ROHINI. Will you all go?

FIRST GARDENER. Yes, all, we have to go instantly. Otherwise we might get into trouble. [They go out.]

ROHINI. I cannot understand their words.... I am afraid. They are scampering off like wild animals that fly just before the bank of a river breaks down into the water.

[Enter KING OF KOSHALA]

KOSHALA. Rohini, do you know where your King and Kanchi have gone?

ROHINI. They are somewhere in the garden, but I could not tell you where.

KOSHALA. I cannot really understand their intentions. I have not done well to put my trust in Kanchi. [Exit.]

ROHINI. What is this dark affair going on amongst these kings? Something dreadful is going to happen soon. Shall I too be drawn into this affair? [Enter AVANTI]

AVANTI. Rohini, do you know where the other princes are?

ROHINI. It is difficult to say which of them is where. The King of Koshala just passed by in this direction.

AVANTI. I am not thinking of Koshala. Where are your King and Kanchi?

ROHINI. I have not seen them for a long time.

AVANTI. Kanchi is always avoiding us. He is certainly planning to deceive us all. I have not done well to put my hand in this imbroglio. Friend, could you kindly tell me any way out of this garden?

ROHINI. I have none.

AVANTI. Is there no man here who will show me the way out?

ROHINI. The servants have all left the garden.

AVANTI. Why did they do so?

ROHINI. I could not exactly understand what they meant. They said the King had commanded them to leave the garden at once.

AVANTI. King? Which King? Rohini They could not say exactly.

AVANTI. This does not sound well. I shall have to find a way out at any cost. I cannot stay here a single moment more. [Goes out hurriedly.]

ROHINI. Where shall I find the King? When I gave him the flowers the Queen had sent, he did not seem much interested in me at the time; but ever since that hour he has been showering gifts and presents on me. This causeless generosity makes me more afraid.... Where are the birds flying at such an hour of the night? What has frightened them all of a sudden? This is not the usual time of their flight, certainly, ... Why is the Queen's pet deer running that way? Chapata! Chapata! She does not even hear my call. I have never seen a night like this! The horizon on every side suddenly becomes red, like a madman's eye! The sun seems to be setting at this untimely hour on all sides at the same time. What madness of the Almighty is this! ... Oh, I am frightened! ... Where shall I find the King?

SCENE VII

[At the Door of the QUEEN'S Palace]

"KING". What is this you have done, Kanchi?

KANCHI. I wanted to fire only this part of the garden near the palace. I had no idea that it would spread so quickly on all sides. Tell me, quick, the way out of this garden.

"KING". I can tell you nothing about it. Those who brought us here have all fled away.

KANCHI. You are a native of this country, you must know the way.

"KING". I have never entered these inner royal gardens before.

KANCHI. I won't hear of it, you must show me the way, or I shall split you into halves.

"KING". You may take my life by that means, but it would be a very precarious method of finding the way out of this garden.

KANCHI. Why were you, then, going about saying that you were the King of this country?

"KING". I am not the King, I am not the King. [Throwing himself on the ground with folded hands.] Where art thou, my King? Save me, oh, save me! I am a rebel, punish me, but do not kill me!

KANCHI. What is the use of shouting and cringing to the empty air? It is a much better way of spending the time to search for the way.

"KING". I shall lie down here, I shall not move an inch. Come what will, I shall not complain.

KANCHI. I will not allow all this nonsense. If I am to be burnt to death, you will be my companion to the very end.

FROM THE OUTSIDE. Oh, save us, save us, our King! The fire is on all sides of us!

KANCHI. Fool, get up, lose no more time.

SUDARSHANA. [entering] King, O my King! save me, save me from death! I am surrounded by fire.

"KING". Who is the King? I am no King.

SUDARSHANA. You are not the King?

"KING". No, I am a hypocrite, I am a scoundrel. [Flinging his crown on the ground.] Let my deception and hypocrisy be shattered into dust! [Goes out with KANCHI.]

SUDARSHANA. No King! He is not the King? Then, O thou God of fire, burn me, reduce me to ashes! I shall throw myself into thy hands, O thou great purifier; burn to ashes my shame, my longing, my desire.

ROHINI. [entering] Queen, where are you going? All your inner chambers are shrouded in raging fire, do you not enter there.

SUDARSHANA. Yes! I will enter those burning chambers! It is the fire of my death! [Enters the Palace.]

SCENE VIII

[The Dark Room. The KING and SUDARSRANA]

KING. Do not be afraid, you have no cause for fear. The fire will not reach this room.

SUDARSHANA. I have no fear, but oh, shame has accompanied me like a raging fire. My face, my eyes, my heart, every part of my body is being scorched and burnt by its flames.

KING. It will be some time before you get over this burning.

SUDARSHANA. This fire will never cease-will never cease!

KING. Do not be despondent, Queen!

SUDARSHANA. O King, I shall not hide anything from you.... I have another's garland round my neck.

KING. That garland, too, is mine, how else could he get it? He stole it from my room.

SUDARSHANA. But it is *his* gift to me: yet I could not fling this garland away! When the fire came roaring on all sides of me, I thought of throwing this garland into the fire. But no, I could not. My mind whispered, "Let that garland be on you in your death." ... What fire is this, O King, into which I, who had come out to see you, leaped like a moth that cannot resist the flame? What a pain is this, oh, what agony! The fire keeps burning as fiercely as ever, but I go on living within its flames!

KING. But you have seen me at last, your desire has been fulfilled.

SUDARSHANA. But did I seek to see you in the midst of this fearful doom? I know not what I saw, but my heart is still beating fast with fear.

KING. What did you see?

SUDARSHANA. Terrible, oh, it was terrible! I am afraid even to think of it again. Black, black, oh, thou art black like the everlasting night! I only looked on thee for one dreadful instant. The blaze of the fire fell on your features, you looked like the awful night when a comet swings fearfully into our ken, oh, then I closed my eyes, I could not look on you anymore. Black as the threatening storm-cloud, black as the shoreless sea with the spectral red tint of twilight on its tumultuous waves!

KING. Have I not told you before that one cannot bear my sight unless one is already prepared for me? One would want to run away from me to the ends of the earth. Have I not seen this times without number? That is why I wanted to reveal myself to you slowly and gradually, not all too sudden.

SUDARSHANA. But sin came and destroyed all your hopes, the very possibility of a union with you has now become unthinkable to me.

KING. It will be possible in time, my Queen. The utter and bleak blackness that has to-day shaken you to your soul with fear will one day be your solace and salvation. What else can my love exist for?

SUDARSHANA. It cannot be, it is not possible. What will your love only do? *My* love has now turned away from you. Beauty has cast its spell on me, this frenzy, this intoxication will never leave me, it has dazzled and fired my eyes, it has thrown its golden glamour over my very dreams! I have told you all now, punish me as you like.

KING. The punishment has already begun.

SUDARSHANA. But if you do not cast me off. I will leave you

KING. You have the utmost liberty to do as you like.

SUDARSHANA. I cannot bear your presence! My heart is angry at you. Why did you but what have you done to me? ... Why are you like this? Why did they tell me you were fair and handsome? Thou art black, black as night, I shall never, I can never, like you. I have seen what I love, it is soft as cream, delicate as the *shirisha* flower, beautiful as a butterfly.

KING. It is false as a mirage, empty as a bubble.

SUDARSHANA. Let it be, but I cannot stand near you, I simply cannot! I must fly away from here. Union with you, it cannot be possible! It cannot be anything but a false union, my mind must inevitably turn away from you.

KING. Will you not even try a little?

SUDARSHANA. I have been trying since yesterday but the more I try, the more rebellious does my heart become. If I stay with you I shall constantly be pursued and hounded by the thought that I am impure, that I am false and faithless.

KING. Well then, you can go as far from me as you like.

SUDARSHANA. I cannot fly away from you, just because you do not prevent my going. Why do you not hold me back, hold me by the hair, saying, "You shall not go"? Why do you not strike me? Oh, punish me, strike me, beat me with violent hands! But your unresisting silence makes me wild, oh, I cannot bear it!

KING. How do you think that I am really silent? How do you know that I am not trying to keep you back?

SUDARSHANA. Oh, no, no ! I cannot bear this, tell me aloud, command me with the voice of thunder, compel me with words that will drown everything else in my ears, do not let me off so easily, so mildly!

KING. I shall leave you free, but why should I let you break away from me?

SUDARSHANA. You will not let me? Well then, I must go!

KING. Go then!

SUDARSHANA. Then I am not to blame at all. You could have held me back by force, but you did not! You have not hindered me, and now I shall go away. Command your sentinels to prevent my going.

KING. No one will stand in your way. You can go as free as the broken storm-cloud driven by the tempest.

SUDARSHANA. I can resist no more, something in me is impelling me forward, I am breaking away from my anchor! Perhaps I shall sink, but I shall return no more. [She rushes out.]

[Enter SURANGAMA, who sings]

SURANGAMA. What will of thine is this that sends me afar! Again shall I come back at thy feet from all my wanderings. It is thy love that feigns this neglect, thy caressing hands are pushing me away, to draw me back to thy arms again! O my King, what is this game that thou art playing throughout thy kingdom?

SUDARSHANA. [re-entering] King, O King!

SURANGAMA. He has gone away.

SUDARSHANA. Gone away? Well then, ... then he has cast me off for good! I have come back, but he could not wait a single instant for me! Very well, then, I am now perfectly free. Surangama, did he ask you to keep me back?

SURANGAMA. No, he said nothing.

SUDARSHANA. Why should he say anything? Why should he care for me? ... I am then free, perfectly free. But, Surangama, I wanted to ask one thing of the King, but could not utter it in his presence. Tell me if he has punished the prisoners with death.

SURANGAMA. Death? My King never punishes with death.

SUDARSHANA. What has he done to them, then?

SURANGAMA. He has set them at liberty. Kanchi has acknowledged his defeat and gone back to his kingdom.

SUDARSHANA. Ah, what a relief!

SURANGAMA. My Queen, I have one prayer to make to you.

SUDARSHANA. You will not have to utter your prayer in words, Surangama. Whatever jewellery and ornaments the King gave me, I leave to you, I am not worthy to wear them now.

SURANGAMA. No, I do not want them, my Queen. My master has never given me any ornaments to wear, my unadorned plainness is good enough for me. He has not given me anything of which I can boast before people.

SUDARSHANA. What do you want of me then?

SURANGAMA. I too shall go with you, my Queen.

SUDARSHANA. Consider what you are saying; you are wanting to leave your master. What a prayer for you to make!

SURANGAMA. I shall not go far from him, when you are going out unguarded he will be with you, close by your side.

SUDARSHANA. You are talking nonsense, my child. I wanted to take Rohini with me, but she would not come. What gives you courage enough to wish to come with me?

SURANGAMA. I have got neither courage nor strength. But I shall go, courage will come of itself, and strength too will come.

SUDARSHANA. No, I cannot take you with me; your presence will constantly remind me of my shame; I shall not be able to endure that.

SURANGAMA. O my Queen, I have made all your good and all your evil my own as well; will you treat me as a stranger still? I must go with you.

SCENE IX

[The KING OF KANYA KUBJA, father of SUDARSHANA, and his MINISTER]

KING OF KANYA KUBJA. I heard everything before her arrival.

MINISTER. The princess is waiting alone outside the city gates on the bank of the river. Shall I send people to welcome her home?

KING OF KANYA KUBJA. What! She who has faithlessly left her husband, do you propose trumpeting her infamy and shame to every one by getting up a show for her?

MINISTER. Shall I then make arrangements for her residence at the palace?

KING OF KANYA KUBJA. You will do nothing of the sort. She has left her place as the Empress of her own accord, here she will have to work as a maid-servant if she wants to stay in my house.

MINISTER. It will be hard and bitter to her, Your Highness.

KING OF KANYA KUBJA. If I seek to save her from her sufferings, then I am not worthy to be her father.

MINISTER. I shall arrange everything as you wish, Your Highness.

KING OF KANYA KUBJA. Let it be kept a secret that she is my daughter; otherwise we shall all be in an awful trouble.

MINISTER. Why do you fear such disaster, Your Highness?

KING OF KANYA KUBJA. When woman swerves from the right path, then she appears fraught with the direst calamity. You do not know with what deadly fear this daughter of mine has inspired me, she is coming to my home laden with peril and danger.

SCENE X

[Inner Apartments of the Palace. SUDARSHANA and SURANGAMA]

SUDARSHANA. Go away from me, Surangama! A deadly anger rages within me, I cannot bear anybody, it makes me wild to see you so patient and submissive.

SURANGAMA. Whom are you angry with?

SUDARSHANA. I do not know; but I wish to see everything destroyed and convulsed in ruin and disaster! I left my place on the throne as the Empress in a moment's time. Did I lose my all to sweep the dust, to sweat and slave in this dismal hole? Why do the torches of mourning not flare up for me all over the world? Why does not the earth quake and tremble? Is my fall but the unobserved dropping of the puny bean-flower?

Is it not more like the fall of a glowing star, whose fiery blazon bursts the heavens asunder?

SURANGAMA. A mighty forest only smokes and smoulders before it bursts into a conflagration: the time has not come yet.

SUDARSHANA. I have thrown my queen's honour and glory to the dust and winds but is there no human being who will come out to meet my desolate soul here? Alone, oh, I am fearfully, terribly alone!

SURANGAMA. You are not alone.

SUDARSHANA. Surangama, I shall not keep anything from you. When he set the palace on fire, I could not be angry with him. A great inward joy set my heart a-flutter all the while. What a stupendous crime! What glorious prowess! It was this courage that made me strong and fired my own spirits. It was this terrible joy that enabled me to leave everything behind me in a moment's time. But is it all my imagination only? Why is there no sign of his coming anywhere?

SURANGAMA. He of whom you are thinking did not set fire to the palace, it is the King of Kanchi who did it.

SUDARSHANA. Coward! But is it possible? So handsome, so bewitching, and yet no manhood in him! Have I deceived myself for the sake of such a worthless creature? O shame! Fie on me! ... But, Surangama, don't you think that your King should yet have come to take me back? [SURANGAMA remains silent.] You think I am anxious to go back? Never! Even if the King really came I should not have returned. Not even once did he forbid me to come away, and I found all the doors wide open to let me out! And the stony and dusty road over which I walked, it was nothing to it that a queen was treading on it. It is hard and has no feelings, like your King; the meanest beggar is the same to it as the highest Empress. You are silent! Well, I tell you, your King's behaviour is mean, brutal, shameful!

SURANGAMA. Every one knows that my King is hard and pitiless no one has ever been able to move him.

SUDARSHANA. Why do you, then, call him day and night?

SURANGAMA. May he ever remain hard and relentless like rock, may my tears and prayers never move him! Let my sorrows be ever mine only and may his glory and victory be for ever!

SUDARSHANA. Surangama, look! A cloud of dust seems to rise over the eastern horizon across the fields.

SURANGAMA. Yes, I see it.

SUDARSHANA. Is that not like the banner of a chariot?

SURANGAMA. Indeed, a banner it is.

SUDARSHANA. Then he is coming. He has come at last!

SURANGAMA. Who is coming?

SUDARSHANA. Our King, who else? How could he live without me? It is a wonder how he could hold out even for these days.

SURANGAMA. No, no, this cannot be the King.

SUDARSHANA. "No," indeed! As if you know everything! Your King is hard, stony, pitiless, isn't he? Let us see how hard he can be. I knew from the beginning that he would come that he would have to rush after me. But remember, Surangama, I never for a single moment asked him to come. You will see how I make your King confess his defeat to me! Just go out, Surangama, and let me know everything. [SURANGAMA goes out.] But shall I go if he comes and asks me to return with him? Certainly not! I will not go! Never!

[Enter SURANGAMA]

SURANGAMA. It is not the King, my Queen.

SUDARSHANA. Not the King? Are you quite sure? What! he has not come yet?

SURANGAMA. No, my King never raises so much dust when he comes. Nobody can know when he comes at all.

SUDARSHANA. Then this is -

SURANGAMA. The same: he is coming with the King of Kanchi.

SUDARSHANA. Do you know his name?

SURANGAMA. His name is Suvarna.

SUDARSHANA. It is he, then. I thought, "I am lying here like waste refuse and offal, which no one cares even to touch." But my hero is coming now to release me. Did you know Suvarna?

SURANGAMA. When I was at my father's home, in the gambling den

SUDARSHANA. No, no, I won't hear anything of him from you. He is my own hero, my only salvation. I shall know him without your telling stories about him. But just see, a nice man your King is! He did not care to come to rescue me from even this degradation. You cannot blame me after this. I could not have waited for him all my life here, toiling ignominiously like a bondslave. I shall never have *your* meekness and submissiveness.

SCENE XI

[Encampment]

KANCHI. [To KANYA KUBJA'S MESSENGER.] Tell your King that he need not receive us exactly as his guests. We are on our way back to our kingdoms, but we are waiting to rescue Queen Sudarshana from the servitude and degradation to which she is condemned here.

MESSENGER. Your Highness, you will remember that the princess is in her father's house.

KANCHI. A daughter may stay in her father's home only so long as she remains unmarried.

MESSENGER. But her connections with her father's family remain intact still.

KANCHI. She has abjured all such relations now.

MESSENGER. Such relationship can never be abjured, Your Highness, on this side of death: it may remain in abeyance at times, but can never be wholly broken up.

KANCHI. If the King chooses not to give up his daughter to me on peaceful terms, our *Kshatriya* code of righteousness will oblige me to employ force. You may take this as my last word.

MESSENGER. Your Highness, do not forget that our King too is bound by the same code. It is idle to expect that he will deliver up his daughter by merely hearing your threats.

KANCHI. Tell your King that I have come prepared for such an answer. [MESSENGER goes out.]

SUVARNA. King of Kanchi, it seems to me that we are daring too much.

KANCHI. What pleasure would there be in this adventure if it were otherwise?

SUVARNA. It does not cost much courage to challenge Kanya Kubja but ...

KANCHI. If you once begin to be afraid of "but," you will hardly find a place in this world safe enough for you.

[Enter a SOLDIER]

SOLDIER. Your Highness! I have just received the news that the Kings of Koshala, Avanti, and Kalinga are coming this way with their armies. [Exit.]

KANCHI. Just what I was afraid of! The report of Sudarshana's flight has spread abroad, now we are going to be in for a general scramble which is sure to end in smoke.

SUVARNA. It is useless now, Your Highness. These are not good tidings. I am perfectly certain that it is our Emperor himself who has secretly spread the report everywhere.

KANCHI. Why, what good will it bring him?

SUVARNA. The greedy ones will tear one another to pieces in the general rivalry and scramble and he will take advantage of the situation to go back with the booty.

KANCHI. Now it becomes clear why your King never shows himself. His trick is to multiply himself on every side, fear makes him visible everywhere. But I will still maintain that your King is but an empty fraud from top to bottom.

SUVARNA. But, please Your Highness, will you have the kindness to let me off?

KANCHI. I cannot let you go, I have some use for you in this affair.

[Enter a SOLDIER]

SOLDIER. Your Highness, Virat, Panchal, and Vidarbha too have come. They have encamped on the other side of the river.[Exit.]

KANCHI. In the beginning we must all fight together. Let the battle with Kanya Kubja first be over, then we shall find some way out of the difficulty.

SUVARNA. Please do not drag me into your plans, I shall be happy if you leave me alone, I am a poor, mean creature, nothing can -

KANCHI. Look here, king of hypocrites, ways and means are never of a very exalted order, roads and stairs and so forth are always to be trodden under our feet. The advantage of utilising men like you in our plans is that we have to make use of no mask or illusion. But if I were to consult my prime minister, it would be absurd for me to call theft by any name less dignified than public benefit. I will go now, and move the princes about like pawns on the chessboard; the game cannot evidently go on if all the chessmen propose moving like kings!

SCENE XII

[Interior of the Palace]

SUDARSHANA. Is the fight still going on?

SURANGAMA. As fiercely as ever.

SUDARSHANA. Before going out to the battle my father came to me and said, "You have come away from one King, but you have drawn seven Kings after you: I have a mind to cut you up into seven pieces and distribute them among the princes. It would have been well if he did so. Surangama!

SURANGAMA. Yes?

SUDARSHANA. If your King had the power to save me, could my present state have left him unmoved?

SURANGAMA. My Queen, why do you ask me? Have I the power to answer for my King? I know my understanding is dark; that is why I never dare to judge him.

SUDARSHANA. Who have joined in this fight?

SURANGAMA. All the seven princes.

SUDARSHANA. No one else?

SURANGAMA. Suvarna attempted to escape, in secret before the fight began but Kanchi has kept him a prisoner in his camps.

SUDARSHANA. Oh, I should have been dead long ago! But, O King, my King, if you had come and helped my father, your fame would have been none the less! It would have become brighter and higher. Are you quite sure, Surangama, that he has not come?

SURANGAMA. I know nothing for certain.

SUDARSHANA. But since I came here I have felt suddenly many a time as if somebody were playing on a *vina* below my window.

SURANGAMA. There is nothing impossible in the idea that somebody indulges his taste for music there.

SUDARSHANA. There is a deep thicket below my window, I try to find out who it is every time I hear the music, but I can see nothing distinctly.

SURANGAMA. Perhaps some wayfarer rests in the shade and plays on the instrument.

SUDARSHANA. It may be so, but my old window in the palace comes back to my memory. I used to come after dressing in the evening and stand at my window, and out of the blank darkness of our lampless meeting-place used to stream forth strains and songs and melodies, dancing and vibrating in endless succession and overflowing profusion, like the passionate exuberance of a ceaseless fountain!

SURANGAMA. O deep and sweet darkness! the profound and mystic darkness whose servant I was!

SUDARSHANA. Why did you come away with me from that room?

SURANGAMA. Because I knew he would follow us and take us back.

SUDARSHANA. But no, he will not come, he has left us for good. Why should he not?

SURANGAMA. If he can leave us like that, then we have no need of him. Then he does not exist for us: then that dark chamber is totally empty and void, no vina ever breathed its music there, none called you or me in that chamber; then everything has been a delusion and an idle dream.

[Enter the DOORKEEPER]

SUDARSHANA. Who are you?

DOORKEEPER. I am the porter of this palace.

SUDARSHANA. Tell me quickly what you have got to say.

DOORKEEPER. Our King has been taken prisoner.

SUDARSHANA. Prisoner? O Mother Earth! [Faints.]

SCENE XIII

[KING OF KANCHI and SUVARNA]

SUVARNA. You say, then, that there will be no more necessity of any fight amongst yourselves?

KANCHI. No, you need not be afraid. I have made all the princes agree that he whom the Queen accepts as her husband will have her, and the others will have to abandon all further struggle.

SUVARNA. But you must have done with me now, Your Highness, so I beg to be let off now. Unfit as I am for anything, the fear of impending danger has unnerved me and stunned my intellect. You will therefore find it difficult to put me to any use.

KANCHI. You will have to sit there as my umbrella-holder.

SUVARNA. Your servant is ready for anything; but of what profit will that be to you?

KANCHI. My man, I see that your weak intellect cannot go with a high ambition in you. You have no notion yet with what favour the Queen looked upon you. After all, she cannot possibly throw the bridal garland on an umbrella-bearer's neck in a company of princes, and yet, I know, she will not be able to turn her mind away from you. So on all accounts this garland will fall under the shade of my regal umbrella.

SUVARNA. Your Highness, you are entertaining dangerous imaginings about me. I pray you, please do not implicate me in the toils of such groundless notions. I beg Your Highness most humbly, pray set me at liberty.

KANCHI. As soon as my object is attained, I shall not keep you one moment from your liberty. Once the end is attained, it is futile to burden oneself with the means.

SCENE XIV

[SUDARSHANA and SURANGAMA at the Window]

SUDARSHANA. Must I go to the assembly of the princes, then? Is there no other means of saving father's life?

SURANGAMA. The King of Kanchi has said so.

SUDARSHANA . Are these the words worthy of a King? Did he say so with his own lips?

SURANGAMA. No, his messenger, Suvarna, brought this news.

SUDARSHANA. Woe, woe is me!

SURANGAMA. And he produced a few withered flowers and said, "Tell your Queen that the drier and more withered these souvenirs of the Spring Festival become, the fresher and more blooming do they grow within in my heart."

SUDARSHANA. Stop! Tell me no more. Do not torment me any more.

SURANGAMA. Look! There sit all the princes in the great assembly. He who has no ornament on his person, except a single garland of flowers round his crown, he is the King of Kanchi. And he who holds the umbrella over his head, standing behind him, that is Suvarna.

SUDARSHANA. Is that Suvarna? Are you quite certain?

SURANGAMA. Yes, I know him well.

SUDARSHANA. Can it be that it is this man that I saw the other day? No, no, I saw something mingled and transfused and blended with light and darkness, with wind and perfume, no, no, it cannot be he; that is not he.

SURANGAMA. But every one admits that he is exceedingly beautiful to look at.

SUDARSHANA. How could that beauty fascinate me? Oh, what shall I do to purge my eyes of their pollution?

SURANGAMA. You will have to wash them in that bottomless darkness.

SUDARSHANA. But tell me, Surangama, why does one make such mistakes?

SURANGAMA. Mistakes are but the preludes to their own destruction.

MESSENGER. [entering] Princess, the Kings are waiting for you in the hall. [Exit.]

SUDARSHANA. Surangama, bring me the veil. [SURANGAMA goes out.] O King, my only King! You have left me alone, and you have been but just in doing so. But will you not know the inmost truth within my soul? [Taking out a dagger from within her bosom.] This body of mine has received a stain, I shall make a sacrifice of it to-day in the dust of the hall, before all these princes! But shall I never be able to tell you that I know of no stain of faithlessness within the hidden chambers of my heart? That dark chamber where you would come to meet me lies cold and empty within my bosom to-day but, O my Lord! none has opened its doors, none has entered it but you, O King! Will you never come again to open those doors? Then, let death come, for it is dark like yourself, and its features are beautiful as yours . It is you, it is yourself, O King!

SCENE XV

[The Gathering of the PRINCES]

VIDARBHA. King of Kanchi, how is it that you have not got a single piece of ornament on your person?

KANCHI. Because I entertain no hopes at all, my friend. Ornaments would but double the shame of my defeat.

KALINGA. But your umbrella-bearer seems to have made up for that, he is loaded with gold and jewellery all over.

VIRAT. The King of Kanchi wants to demonstrate the futility and inferiority of outer beauty and grandeur. Vanity of his prowess has made him discard all outer embellishments from his limbs.

KOSLIALA. I am quite up to his trickery; he is seeking to prove his own dignity, maintaining a severe plainness among the bejewelled princes.

PANCHALA. I cannot commend his wisdom in this matter. Every one knows that a woman's eyes are like a moth in that they fling themselves headlong on the glare and glitter of jewel and gold.

KALINGA. But how long shall we have to wait more?

KANCHI. Do not grow impatient, King of Kalinga, sweet are the fruits of delay.

KALINGA. If I were sure of the fruit I could have endured it. It is because my hopes of tasting the fruit are extremely precarious that my eagerness to have a sight of her breaks through all bounds.

KANCHI. But you are young still, abandoned hope comes back to you again and again like a shameless woman at your age: we, however, have long passed that stage.

KOSHALA. Kanchi, did you feel as if something shook your seat just now? Is it an earthquake?

KANCHI. Earthquake? I do not know.

VIDARBHA. Or perhaps some other prince is coming with his army.

KALINGA. There is nothing against your theory except that we should have first heard the news from some herald or messenger in that case.

VIDARBHA. I cannot regard this as a very auspicious omen.

KANCHI. Everything looks inauspicious to the eye of fear.

VIDARBHA. I fear none except Fate, before which courage or heroism is as futile as it is absurd.

PANCHALA. Vidarbha, do not darken to-day's happy proceedings with your unwelcome prognostications.

KANCHI. I never take the unseen into account till it has become "seen."

VIDARBHA. But then it might be too late to do anything.

PANCHALA. Did we not all of us start at a specially auspicious moment?

VIDARBHA. Do you think you insure against every possible risk by starting at auspicious moments? It looks as if -

KANCHI. You had better let the "as if" alone: though our own creation, it often proves our ruin and destruction.

KALINGA. Isn't that music somewhere outside?

PANCHALA. Yes, it sounds like music, sure enough.

KANCHI. Then at last it must be the Queen Sudarshana who is approaching near. [Aside to SUVARNA.] Suvarna, you must not hide and cower behind me like that. Mind, the umbrella in your hand is shaking!

[Enter GRANDFATHER, dressed as a warrior]

KALINGA. Who is that? Who are you?

PANCHALA. Who is this that dares to enter this hall without being invited?

VIRAT. Amazing impudence! Kalinga, just prevent the fellow from advancing further.

KALINGA. You are all my superiors in age, you are fitter to do that than myself.

VIDARBHA. Let us hear what he has to say.

GRANDFATHER. The KING has come.

VIDARBHA. [starting] King?

PANCHALA. Which King?

KALINGA. Where does he come from?

GRANDFATHER. My King!

VIRAT. Your King?

KALINGA. Who is he?

KOSHALA. What do you mean?

GRANDFATHER. You all know whom I mean. He has come.

VIDARBHA. He has come?

KOSHALA. With what intention?

GRANDFATHER. He has summoned you all to come to him.

KANCHI. Summoned us, indeed? In what terms has he been pleased to summon us?

GRANDFATHER. You can take his call in any way you like, there is none to prevent you, he is prepared to make all kinds of welcome to suit your various tastes.

VIRAT. But who are you?

GRANDFATHER. I am one of his generals.

KANCHI. Generals? It is a lie! Do you think of frightening us? Do you imagine that I cannot see through your disguise? We all know you well and you pose as a "general" before us!

GRANDFATHER. You have recognised me to perfection. Who is so unworthy as I to bear my King's commands? And yet it is he who has invested me with these robes of a general and sent me here: he has chosen me before greater generals and mightier warriors.

KANCHI. All right, we shall go to observe the proprieties and amenities on a fitting occasion but at present we are in the midst of a pressing engagement. He will have to wait till this little function is over.

GRANDFATHER. When he sends out his call he does not wait.

KOSHALA. I shall obey his call; I am going at once.

VIDARBHA. Kanchi, I cannot agree with you in your proposal to wait till this function is over. I am going.

KALINGA. You are older than I am, I shall follow you.

PANCHALA. Look behind you, Prince of Kanchi, your regal umbrella is lying in the dust: you have not noticed when your umbrella-holder has stolen away.

KANCHI. All right, general. I too am going but not to do him homage. I go to fight him on the battle-ground.

GRANDFATHER. You will meet my King in the field of battle: that is no mean place for your reception.

VIRAT. Look here, friends, perhaps we are all flying before an imagined terror, it looks as if the King of Kanchi will have the best of it.

PANCHALA. Possibly, when the fruit is so near the hand, it is cowardly and foolish to go away without plucking it.

KALINGA. It is better to join the King of Kanchi. He cannot be without a definite plan and purpose when he is doing and daring so much.

SCENE XVI

[SUDARSHANA and SURANGAMA]

SUDARSHANA. The fight is over now. When will the King come?

SURANGAMA. I do not know myself: I am also looking forward to his coming.

SUDARSHANA. I feel such a throb of joy, Surangama, that my breast is positively aching. But I am dying with shame too; how shall I show my face to him?

SURANGAMA. Go to him in utmost humility and resignation, and all shame will vanish in a moment.

SUDARSHANA. I cannot help confessing that I have met with my uttermost defeat for all the rest of my life. But pride made me claim the largest share in his love so long. Every one used to say I had such wonderful beauty, such graces and virtues; every one used to say that the King showed unlimited kindness towards me, this is what makes it difficult for me to bend my heart in humility before him.

SURANGAMA. This difficulty, my Queen, will pass off.

SUDARSHANA. Oh, yes, it will pass, the day has arrived for me to humble myself before the whole world. But why does not the King come to take me back? What more is he waiting for yet?

SURANGAMA. Have I not told you my King is cruel and hard, very hard indeed?

SUDARSHANA. Go out, Surangama, and bring me news of him.

SURANGAMA. I do not know where I should go to get any news of him. I have asked Grandfather to come; perhaps when he comes we shall hear something from him.

SUDARSHANA. Alack, my evil fate! I have been reduced to asking others to hear about my own King!

[Transciber's note: Alack should probably be replaced with Alas.]

[Enter GRANDFATHER]

SUDARSHANA. I have heard that you are my King's friend, so accept my obeisance and give me your blessings.

GRANDFATHER. What are you doing, Queen? I never accept anybody's obeisance. My relation with every one is only that of comradeship.

SUDARSHANA. Smile on me, then give me good news. Tell me when the King is coming to take me back.

GRANDFATHER. You ask me a hard question, indeed! I hardly understand yet the ways of my friend. The battle is over, but no one can tell where he is gone.

SUDARSHANA. Is he gone away, then?

GRANDFATHER. I cannot find any trace of him here.

SUDARSHANA. Has he gone? And do you call such a person your friend?

GRANDFATHER. That is why he gets people's abuse as well as suspicion. But my King simply does not mind it in the least.

SUDARSHANA. Has he gone away? Oh, oh, how hard, how cruel, how cruel! He is made of stone, he is hard as adamant! I tried to move him with my own bosom, my breast is torn and bleeding but him I could not move an inch! Grandfather, tell me, how can you manage with such a friend?

GRANDFATHER. I have known him now, I have known him through my griefs and joys, he can make me weep no more now.

SUDARSHANA. Will he not let me know him also?

GRANDFATHER. Why, he will, of course. Nothing else will satisfy him.

SUDARSHANA. Very well, I shall see how hard he can be! I shall stay here near the window without saying a word; I shall not move an inch; let me see if he will not come!

GRANDFATHER. You are young still, you can afford to wait for him; but to me, an old man, a moment's loss is a week. I must set out to seek him whether I succeed or not.[Exit.]

SUDARSHANA. I do not want him, I will not seek him! Surangama, I have no need of your King! Why did he fight with the princes? Was it for me at all? Did he want to show off his prowess and strength? Go away from here, I cannot bear your sight. He has humbled me to the dust, and is not satisfied still!

SCENE XVII

[A Band of CITIZENS]

FIRST CITIZEN. When so many Kings met together, we thought we were going to have some big fun; but somehow everything took such a turn that nobody knows what happened at all!

SECOND CITIZEN. Did you not see, they could not come to an agreement among themselves? every one distrusted every one else.

THIRD CITIZEN. None kept to their original plans; one wanted to advance, another thought it better policy to recede; some went to the right, others made a rush to the left: how can you call that a fight?

FIRST CITIZEN. They had no eye to real fighting, each had his eye on the others.

SECOND CITIZEN. Each was thinking, "Why should I die to enable others to reap the harvest?"

THIRD CITIZEN. But you must all admit that Kanchi fought like a real hero.

FIRST CITIZEN. He for a long time after his defeat seemed loth to acknowledge himself beaten.

SECOND CITIZEN. He was at last fixed in the chest by a deadly missile.

THIRD CITIZEN. But before that he did not seem to realise that he had been losing ground at every step.

FIRST CITIZEN. As for the other Kings, well, nobody knows where they fled, leaving poor Kanchi alone in the field.

SECOND CITIZEN. But I have heard that he is not dead yet.

THIRD CITIZEN. No, the physicians have saved him but he will carry the mark of his defeat on his breast till his dying day.

FIRST CITIZEN. None of the other Kings who fled has escaped; they have all been taken prisoners. But what sort of justice is this that was meted out to them?

SECOND CITIZEN. I heard that every one was punished except Kanchi, whom the judge placed on his right on the throne of justice, putting a crown on his head.

THIRD CITIZEN. This beats all mystery hollow.

SECOND CITIZEN. This sort of justice, to speak frankly, strikes us as fantastic and capricious.

FIRST CITIZEN. Just so. The greatest offender is certainly the King of Kanchi; as for the others, greed of gain now pressed them to advance, now they drew back in fear.

THIRD CITIZEN. What kind of justice is this, I ask? It is as if the tiger got scot-free, while his tail got cut off.

SECOND CITIZEN. If I were the judge, do you think Kanchi would be whole and sound at this hour? There would be nothing left of him altogether.

THIRD CITIZEN. They are great, high justices, my friends; their brains are of a different stamp from ours.

FIRST CITIZEN. Have they got any brains at all, I wonder? They simply indulge their sweet whims as there are none to say anything to them from above.

SECOND CITIZEN. Whatever you may say, if we had the governing power in our hands we should certainly have carried on the government much better than this.

THIRD CITIZEN. Can there be any real doubts about that? That of course goes without saying.

SCENE XVIII

[The Street. GRANDFATHER and KANCHI]

GRANDFATHER. What, Prince of Kanchi, you here!

KANCHI. Your King has sent me on the road.

GRANDFATHER. That is a settled habit with him.

KANCHI. And now, no one can get a glimpse of him.

GRANDFATHER. That too is one of his amusements.

KANCHI. But how long more will he elude me like this? When nothing could make me acknowledge him as my King, he came all of a sudden like a terrific tempest, God knows from where and scattered my men and horses and banners in one wild tumult: but now, when I am seeking the ends of the earth to pay him my humble homage, he is nowhere to be seen.

GRANDFATHER. But however big an Emperor he may be, he has to submit to him that yields. But why have you come out at night, Prince?

KANCHI. I still cannot get rid of the feeling of a secret dread of being laughed at by people when they see me meekly doing my homage to your King, acknowledging my defeat.

GRANDFATHER. Such indeed is the people. What would move others to tears only serves to move their empty laughter.

KANCHI. But you too are on the road, Grandfather.

GRANDFATHER. This is my jolly pilgrimage to the land of losing everything.

SINGS.

I am waiting with my all in the hope of losing everything.
I am watching at the roadside for him who turns one out into the open road,
Who hides himself and sees, who loves you unknown to you,
I have given my heart in secret love to him,
I am waiting with my all in the hope of losing everything.

SCENE XIX

[A Road. SUDARSHANA and SURANGAMA]

SUDARSHANA. What a relief, Surangama, what freedom! It is my defeat that has brought me freedom. Oh, what an iron pride was mine! Nothing could move it or soften it. My darkened mind could not in any way be brought to see the plain truth that it was not the King who was to come, it was I who ought to have gone to him. All through yesternight I lay alone on the dusty floor before that window, lay there through the desolate hours and wept! All night the southern winds blew and shrieked and moaned like the pain that was biting at my heart; and all through it I heard the plaintive "Speak, wife!" of the nightbird echoing in the tumult outside! ... It was the helpless wail of the dark night, Surangama!

SURANGAMA. Last night's heavy and melancholy air seemed to hang on for an eternity, oh, what a dismal and gboomy night!

SUDARSHANA. But would you believe it, I seemed to hear the soft strains of the *vina* floating through all that wild din and tumult! Could he play such sweet and tender tunes, he who is so cruel and terrible? The world knows only my indignity and ignominy but none but my own heart could hear those strains that called me through the lone and wailing night. Did you too, Surangama, hear the *vina*? Or was that but a dream of mine?

SURANGAMA. But it is just to hear that same *vina*'s music that I am always by your side. It is for this call of music, which I knew would one day come to dissolve all the barriers of love, that I have all along been listening with an eager ear.

SUDARSHANA. He did at last send me on the open road, I could not withstand his will. When I shall find him, the first words that I shall tell him will be, "I have come of my own will, I have not awaited your coming." I shall say, "For your sake have I trodden the hard and weary roads, and bitter and ceaseless has been my weeping all the way." I shall at least have this pride in me when I meet him.

SURANGAMA. But even that pride will not last. He came before you did, who else could have sent you on the road?

SUDARSHANA. Perhaps he did. As long as a sense of offended pride remained with me, I could not help thinking that he had left me for good; but when I flung my dignity and pride to the winds and came out on the common streets, then it seemed to me that he too had come out: I have been finding him since the moment I was on the road. I have no misgivings now. All this suffering that I have gone through for his sake, the very bitternesss of all this is giving me his company. Ah! yes, he has come,he has held me by the hand, just as he used to do in that chamber of darkness, when, at his touch, all my body would start with a sudden thrill: it is the same, the same touch again! Who says that he is not here? Surangama, can you not see that he has come, in silence and secret? ... Who is that there? Look, Surangama, there is a third traveller of this dark road at this hour of the night.

SURANGAMA. I see, it is the King of Kanchi, my Queen.

SUDARSHANA. King of Kanchi!

SURANGAMA. Don't be afraid, my Queen!

SUDARSHANA. Afraid! Why should I be afraid? The days of fear are gone for ever for me.

KANCHI. [entering] Queen-mother, I see you two on this road! I am a traveller of the same path as yourself. Have no fear of me, O Queen!

SUDARSHANA. It is well, King of Kanchi, that we should be going together, side by side, this is but right. I came on your way when I first left my home, and now I meet you again on my way back. Who could have dreamed that this meeting of ours would augur so well?

KANCHI. But, Queen-mother, it is not meet that you should walk over this road on foot. Will you permit me to get a chariot for you?

SUDARSHANA. Oh, do not say so: I shall never be happy if I could not on my way back home tread on the dust of the road that led me away from my King. I would be deceiving myself if I were now to go in a chariot.

SURANGAMA. King, you too are walking in the dust to-day: this road has never known anybody driving his horse or chariot over it.

SUDARSHANA. When I was the Queen, I stepped over silver and gold, I shall have now to atone for the evil fortune of my birth by walking over dust and bare earth. I could not have dreamed that thus I would meet my King of common earth and dust at every step of mine to-day.

SURANGAMA. Look, my Queen, there on the eastern horizon comes the dawn. We have not long to walk: I see the spires of the golden turrets of the King's palace.

[Enter GRANDFATHER]

GRANDFATHER. My child, it is dawn at last!

SUDARSHANA. Your benedictions have given me Godspeed, and here I am, at last.

GRANDFATHER. But do you see how ill-mannered our King is? He has sent no chariot, no music band, nothing splendid or grand.

SUDARSHANA. Nothing grand, did you say? Look, the sky is rosy and crimson from end to end, the air is full of the welcome of the scent of flowers.

GRANDFATHER. Yes, but however cruel our King may be, we cannot seek to emulate him: I cannot help feeling pain at seeing you in this state, my child. How can we bear to see you going to the King's palace attired in this poor and wretched attire? Wait a little, I am running to fetch you your Queen's garments.

SUDARSHANA. Oh no, no, no! He has taken away those regal robes from me forever, he has attired me in a servant's dress before the eyes of the whole world: what a relief this has been to me! I am his servant now, no longer his Queen. To-day I stand at the feet of all those who can claim any relationship with him.

GRANDFATHER. But your enemies will laugh at you now: how can you bear their derision?

SUDARSHANA. Let their laughter and derision be immortal, let them throw dust at me in the streets: this dust will to-day be the powder with which I shall deck myself before meeting my lord.

GRANDFATHER. After this, we shall say nothing. Now let us play the last game of our Spring Festival instead of the pollen of flowers let the south breeze blow and scatter dust of lowliness in every direction! We shall go to the lord clad in the common grey of the dust. And we shall find him too covered with dust all over. For do you think the people spare him? Even he cannot escape from their soiled and dusty hands, and he does not even care to brush the dirt off his garments.

KANCHI. Grandfather, do not forget me in this game of yours! I also will have to get this royal garment of mine soiled till it is beyond all recognition.

GRANDFATHER. That will not take long, my brother. Now that you have come down so far, you will change your colour in no time. Just look at our Queen, she got into a temper with herself and thought that she could spoil her matchless beauty by flinging away all her ornaments: but this insult to her beauty has made it shine forth in tenfold radiance, and now it is in its unadorned perfection. We hear that our King is all innocent of beauty, that is why he loves all his manifold beauty of form which shines as the very ornament of his breast. And that beauty has to-day taken off its veil and cloak of pride and vanity! What could I not give to be allowed to hear the wonderful music and song that has filled my King's palace to-day!

SURANGAMA. Lo, there rises the sun!

SCENE XX

[The Dark Chamber]

SUDARSHANA. Lord, do not give me back the honour which you once did turn away from me! I am the servant of your feet, I only seek the privilege of serving you.

KING. Will you be able to bear me now?

SUDARSHANA. Oh yes, yes, I shall. Your sigh repelled me because I had sought to find you in the pleasure garden, in my Queen's chambers: there even your meanest servant looks handsomer than you. That fever of longing has left my eyes for ever. You are not beautiful, my lord, you stand beyond all comparisons!

KING. That which can be comparable with me lies within yourself.

SUDARSHANA. If this be so, then that too is beyond comparison. Your love lives in me, you are mirrored in that love, and you see your face reflected in me: nothing of this mine, it is all yours, O lord!

KING. I open the doors of this dark room to-day, the game is finished here! Come, come with me now, come outside *into the light!*

SUDARSHANA. Before I go, let me bow at the feet of my lord of darkness, my cruel, my terrible, my peerless one!

Rabindranath Tagore – A Biography

Rabindranath Tagore (1861-1941) is an Indian poet, playwright, novelist, composer, painter and a national icon of his country. His profuse literary production ranges from collections of poems such as *Manasi* (1890), *Gitanjali* (1910) and Patraput (1936) to drama such as *Visarjan* (1890), *Raja* (1910), *Muktadhara* (1922) and *Chandalika* (1938) and even numerous musical compositions and songs. In addition, Tagore's publications include a number of novels and several volumes of short stories including his widely appreciated *Gora* (1910) along with *Chaturanga* (1916) and *Ghare-Baire* (1916). The latter is one of his many works that were adapted to cinema.

Born in Calcutta, India, to a well-off family, Rabindranath Tagore was raised and educated mainly by servants. His father Devendranath Tagore is a saint and a religious leader of the Adi Dham faith and the Brahmo sect founded by the family's patriarchs. Young Rabindranath Tagore's home was animated by discussions of literary publications, arts, theatrical performances and classical music where most of his 14 siblings were much interested in arts, poetry, music, philosophy and theatre, such as his older sister, Swarnakumari Devi, the renowned Indian novelist, poet and musician.

In addition to such a supportive environment for artistic appreciation and creativity, Tagore's father made him discover language, literature, history and poetry, taking him for long journeys around the country. In 1873, they both left home for the hill station at Dalhousie. Named after the British Governor-General Lord Dalhousie who used to visit it during his summer holidays, the station is surrounded by captivating green hills and heaven-like vistas. During the months spent there, Tagore must have found in the station's assortments of Hindu art and temples, along with the European architecture of its summer residences, a magnificent blending of East and West.

Readers of Tagore's poetry, novels and short stories, such as "The Fruitseller from Kabul," to name but a sample, can surely detect in their imagery and emotional outlets the influence of Dalhousie's breath-taking sceneries and verdure. Tagore's journey with his father was mainly meant to be a necessary stage towards intellectual and moral maturity and individuation. The lessons that the father transmitted to the son in such an inspirational spot were not only meant to be informational lessons but also spiritual ones. Indeed, being a very respected spiritual figure who wished to hand on the torch to younger disciples, Tagore's father inculcated in him mystical yearnings for spiritual knowledge and existential meaning.

It is, however, noteworthy that despite his conspicuous lust for knowledge, Tagore hated the "yoke" of formal education and thought that classroom teaching could only muffle young people's innate and instinctive thirst for discovery and adventure. The two long journeys that he had with his father only reinforced this attitude as they helped nourish his love for nature and the divine. Helped by his father, his brother Hemendranath and the house servants, Tagore studied language, literature, mathematics, geography and history and practiced different sports at home and in the family's manor. When his father sent him to London to study law in 1878, he quickly left University College London and chose to study language, literature and music by himself. Two years later, he travelled back to India without getting the formal degree he was sent for.

Tagore expressed in many an occasion his belief that teaching should arouse curiosity rather than be informative and he strove to put his ideas into practice particularly by founding the Visva-Bharati school, which has now become the Visva-Bharati University, where he established the "brahmacharya" educational system. The main characteristic of Tagore's educational conception was to have teachers incite their students to discover and learn through employing intellectual and spiritual motivational strategies.

As for his writings, Tagore was a genuine prodigy who started weaving his earliest verses by the age of eight in the family's Calcutta residence. A few years later, he pseudonymously published his first collection of poems which was an astounding success to the point that local critics thought the compilation to belong to the 17th-century poet Bhanusimha. He soon shifted to writing short stories and plays to achieve considerable fame in the region. While all his writings were in his native Bengali language, he eventually decided to address Western readers by translating some of his own works into English.

The English versions of his poetic works such as *Manasi* (1890), *Gitimalya* (1914) and mainly what is today considered in the West as his magnum opus, *Gitanjali* (1910), quickly gained ground among Western literary circles. Such works were read, reviewed and prefaced by leading literary figures of the time like William Butler Yeats and Ezra Pound. Tagore soon became an oriental icon who stands for India's literary, spiritual and cultural heritage. In 1913, the relatively small part of his works discovered by the West earned him the Nobel Prize in Literature. In 1915, he was also knighted by the British Crown for his literary achievements.

Once famous in the West, Tagore toured Britain and the United States and lectured in many other European and non-European countries to meet and interact with important celebrities around the world including the celebrated German-born physicist Albert Einstein, Thomas Mann, George Bernard Shaw and H.G. Wells, among many others.

Politically, while Tagore's commitment manifested in his harsh criticism of nationalist extremism and in his avant-garde and reformatory positions at home, he denounced imperialism and advocated universalism and internationalism in the world. In India, he was known for his rejection of the culture of victimhood and for inciting his countrymen to have the courage of assuming the responsibilities of their misfortunes. He saw that salvation could only be realized through education and self-help. In addition to that, Tagore was also socially active in his homeland, supporting students and the poor. As for foreign affairs, Tagore denounced British colonialism and even renounced the honor previously granted by the British Crown in protest against the 1919 Jallianwala Bagh massacre.

Such political views were explicitly expressed in some of Tagore's writings and musical compositions, two of which were chosen by India and Bangladesh as national anthems. His friend Mahatma Gandhi, the celebrated leader of the Indian nationalist movement, expressed his appreciation of these compositions and was said to favor the "Ekla Chalo Re" hymn.

Towards the twilight of his career, Tagore developed new interests, mainly in arts, paintings and sciences. This is mainly expressed in stories like *Se* (1937) and *Tin Sangi* (1940) as well as in his collection of essays entitled *Visva-Parichay* (1937) which represents a literary man's exploration of the fields of astronomy, physics and biology. He even took up drawing and painting at a late age and organized exhibitions of his works in Paris and other cities.

Towards the end of the 1930s, old Rabindranath Tagore's health started to deteriorate until he died on August 7th, 1941, leaving a gigantic oeuvre of numerous volumes of fine poetry, hundreds of texts, short stories, novels, plays, paintings, doodles, more than two thousand songs, two autobiographies and numerous travelogues, essays and lectures.

Tagore's life experience had taught him that divisions between human beings are nothing but an unpleasant mirage. Generally, his oeuvre invites and incites its readers to the exploration of the Other, the exploration of the Self. The following extract from his masterpiece *Gitanjali* may serve as a perfect illustration of Tagore's philosophical vision:

The time that my journey takes is long and the way of it long.
I came out on the chariot of the first gleam of light, and pursued my voyage through the wildernesses of worlds leaving my track on many a star and planet.

It is the most distant course that comes nearest to thyself, and that training is the most intricate which leads to the utter simplicity of a tune. The traveller has to knock at every alien door to come to his own, and one has to wander through all the outer worlds to reach the innermost shrine at the end.

My eyes strayed far and wide before I shut them and said 'Here art thou!'
The question and the cry 'Oh, where?' melt into tears of a thousand
streams and deluge the world with the flood of the assurance 'I am!'
(Song XII)

www.ingramcontent.com/pod-product-compliance
Lightning Source LLC
Chambersburg PA
CBHW061253040426
42444CB00010B/2369